Let Me Count The Ways

POETIC EXPRESSIONS

RICKY R. JONES

Copyright © 2025 Ricky R. Jones

Cover Creation Direction by Sebrina Phillips

All rights reserved. This publication may not be reproduced in any form without permission in writing from the publisher. Unauthorized reproduction of any part of this work is illegal and is punishable by law.

ISBN 978-1-950861-91-0

PRINTED IN THE UNITED STATES OF AMERICA

Wendell, North Carolina

Dedication

To the memory of my beloved brother,
Brian Keith Jones Sr., my closest
family and friends, life experiences,
and of course, my loving inspiration, Sebrina.

Thank you one and all for your unwavering support.
God bless.

Table of Contents

From the Heart of the Author 1
I Am (male proposal) 2
"Are You Now" (female response) 3
Let's Do It 4
I See 5
My Love 6
Inseparable Dreams 7
A Work Of Art 8
!!VICTORY!! 9
Honey 10
Surrender 11
Stubborn Pride 12
Baby Love 13
Words Of Love 14
The Drifter 15
Reach 16
Sacred Blessings 17
Sweetness 18
Mother Dear 19
All Mine 20
Game Over 21
It Is I 22
Mirror Image 23
Love 24
Hearts 25
Unity 26
Distant Lover 27
Special Feelings 28
Only You 29
Cheers 30
Dear Friend 31

Honest	32
Thank You	33
Comfort	34
Destiny	35
Say Yes	36
I Love You	37
It's Me	38
Cinderella	39
She Tried	40
My Girl	41
Sebrina	42
Positive Thoughts	43
Tears Of Joy	44
You Are	45
One Song	46
What If	47
The Question Is	48
Looking Good	49
Hot Showers	50
Have You Ever	51
So Good	52
Always	53
Private Dancer	54
My Vow	55
The Photographic Message	56
Just Saying	57
Love Your Woman	58
Matrimony	59
Smooches	60
Emotional Circumstances	61
True Love	62
Sweet Love	63
Greater Is He	64
Absolutely	65
God Is Love	66

From the Heart of the Author

Humble I am as humble can be
thank you Lord for gifting me
with an ambitious poetic mind
as a published Author now is the time
to exercise my every intention
to bask in success and have my name mentioned
as one of the better poets in this land
I am excited I have so much planned
this my first official poetry book publication
overwhelms my heart with much needed elation
this manuscript is highly favored
with blessings from my Lord and Savior

I Am (male proposal)

I challenge you, sweetheart, to discover a man
who can lift your spirits the way I can
I shall wine you and dine you hold you ever so closely
my affectionate touches will make you feel cozy
I am flowers—I am candy— I am pleasant surprises
I am complimentary gestures, what you need to realize is
I am the guy, the when, the why
my shoulder is yours if you need to cry
I am built to adore you one million times over
I am your modern-day Casanova

"Are You Now" (female response)

Modern-day Cassanova, that sounds sweet
I am the woman most likely to complete
the curious task of loving you whole
and inevitably becoming your someone to hold
I could cry on your shoulder "yes"
Are you positioned to withstand the test
of what it would take to love me right
for my honor, are you willing to fight
I can seize control of your when's and why's
and fulfill them with comforts you have never realized
your kind gestures seem very nice
for the most part, I am somewhat enticed
however, I am a queen you see
who gives you no choice but to fall on one knee
and profess your love to me for life
if you play your cards right, I could be your wife

Let's Do It

Let's gaze into each other's eyes
let's get serious let's compromise
let's focus babe let's understand
the exclusive bond between woman and man
compatibility is our forte
let's not wait let's hope let's pray
let's commit to each other let's kiss let's hug
let's be amazing let's fall in love

I See

The attraction is noticed when you stare
Toward the path of my direction
Your gleaming pupils reflect a glare
I label as pure perfection
To look at you is to love
The quality you recognize
I am irresistibly fond of
The beauty I see in your eyes

My Love

Each moment she is near me
My mind settles with peace
Daily monthly and yearly
Her worth and values increase
All she has to do is smile
And everything is all right
Charm is something she tends to compile,
Morning noon and night
Without her by my side
I lose the will to try
My cheerful preference becomes denied
When she is away, I cry

Inseparable Dreams

Fly with me to paradise
On a journey through lovers' lane
Shall we let the powers of love entice
The trust for each other we've gained
Fly with me to paradise
Encourage my will to enhance
Flatter me with the sugar and spice
Involved with the thrills of romance
Fly with me to paradise
Far beyond and above
Togetherness is a way of life
Upon the wings of love

A Work Of Art

Lately, I have been feeling real good
About the way my life has been going
Precisely like I figured it would
Admiration for you keeps growing
Your influence on my life
Is increasing daily
Obviously, you are outright
The classiest of all ladies
Smiles are as frequent on my face
As dampness on morning dew
Frowns are diminishing without chase
And I owe it all to you

!!VICTORY!!

Deep in the shadows of love
Appear two identities
This apparent truce is made up of
A couple so young and free
Ambitiously they correspond
To blessings brilliantly rendered
Solid ideas of a solemn bond
Relish with sweet surrender
Into the sunset they go
Pinpointing security
The reflection of that sunlight shows
The beginning of you and me

Honey

I long to hold you, kiss you and squeeze you
Serenade you softly and aim to please you
Honey, I want to love you and love you
At this very moment, no one is above you
I need to see you ~ I can't live without you
I guess you can say I am crazy about you
Honey, I'd just as soon give you the world
Simply because you're one classy old girl
I live to say there is seldom a time
When you fail to enter the core of my mind
Honey, I would do anything to make right
A chance to come home to you each night

Surrender

Have I the right to stake a claim
Into the depths of your soul
Are your feelings subject to change
What does our future hold
If for some reason, there is
Talk of another man
Should thoughtless jealous feelings exist
Or should I understand
Have I the right to be
The enforcer of second glances
Am I in position to summon a plea
Tell me, what are my chances

Stubborn Pride

Pride is not worth a dime
It interferes with feelings
All it does is create a line
Between lover's romantic dealings
Whoever created this five-letter word
Certainly doesn't have much going
Or could it be he has not heard
It is better when feelings are showing

Baby Love

I admired you, you captured my heart
brightening my spirits was your role from the start
the reality of spending time with you
always kept me in the fondest of moods
my romantic involvement with you was intense
catering to your every need made sense
I specifically labeled you angel of love
before I lay sleep you were who I thought of
I proclaimed your touch as my reason for passion
and made love to you in desirable fashion
loving you it seemed was my way of life
I even pondered the thought of calling you wife
let me explain, I was under a spell
consumed with infatuation with no room to exhale
imagine the most tragic scenario
establishing compassion for a woman and having to let go
sincerely my feelings for you felt so right
I honestly loved you with all of my might

Words Of Love

Admiration is a sensation when you are the object of
Infatuation; you and me, can we be, do we dare to comfort and
Care; I deserve and admire, just craving the chance to raise the
stakes higher.
This bouquet of flowers says I could spend hours adoring you,
"Cherie Amouring" you, you look so sweet, can I be discrete,
trust me Baby you matter, wanna hear some love chatter, you have the
softest skin, darling where have you been, my search is over, you
are my four-leaf clover, you are a modern-day queen with soft eyes that
gleam, I desire your touch, let me tell you how much.
Be mine anytime, we would wine and dine - constantly blow
each other's mind, we'd be smiling- profiling-the need for love
would start piling; we'd gaze sending rays of love through the
place; we'd take a sip, leave a tip, head for a passionate trip; we'd
go outside, hop in the ride, in each other we would confide.
I would take you home, we'd be alone, take the receiver off the phone.
A romantic explosion is what I am thinking of, if you consent
to giving this notion, a shove, then I can do it, hold me to it, trust
me - completely, I will talk you right through it, a passionate kiss,
give it up I insist, in these arms of mine is where you'll find bliss,
say yes, never no, never stop, always go, look at what you've
done girl, I am starting to grow, go ahead feel, I know you'll be
thrilled, if you are thinking maybe not, go against your own will.
please do not take offense - I am so darn intense, making love to
you in the heat of this moment... makes sense!

The Drifter

I am a very lonely man
I spread my love around
I extend my services throughout the land
Moving from town to town
I guess you can say I'm unstable
I have no place to go
I am absolutely unable
To surface my feelings a glow
I am so discouraged
Unhappy with my fate
I do not even have the courage
To say it is never too late
I am a hostage of desperation
Does anyone hear my cry?
Episodes of aggravation
Provoke my wishes to die
Innocent lady of character
Come forth and bring me life
Whoever you are, I really care
Loneliness cuts like a knife
Oh, Cupid can you brighten
The dim stars I see above
Cast down upon me and enlighten
My negative outlook on Love

Reach

The places we ventured when you were here
Now seem so non-existent
Apparently, I cannot adhere
To worldly pleasures because you are distant
I am lost without the accommodation
Of holding your caring hand
Being with you is an obligation
Designed to increase my life span
Like a programmed robot
To you I am dedicated
Desirably so I feel somewhat
Happily, situated
As passing time accumulates,
I nurse a heart that yearns
Night after night it excessively aches
For the day of your return

Sacred Blessings

GOD created the birds to fly high above the trees
HE multicolored HIS autumn leaves
HE shaped the millions of stars that gleam
HE brightened the moon, what a glorious scene
actually, I could go on forever
miraculous are HIS wondrous endeavors
could it be your heartbeat coupled with mine
is a sacred match dear GOD designed
you obviously are the heavenly devotion
GOD afforded me with to humble my emotions
while enchanted with you peace is achieved
spending time with you helps me believe
GOD made woman for man
to strengthen his will to survive
HE purposely carried out this plan
to keep his stability revived
HE removed from man the rib
that made possible her creation
since then man has learned to live
and acknowledge this relation
you and I for instance
we are HIS ideal pair
the strength of our existence
is showing how much we care
who are we to debate
our Master's vivid views
it appears you have a permanent mate
GOD made me for you

Sweetness

She and me at one time were a We
Circumstances prevailed and we could no longer be
Her role in my life was kind of soothing
To be honest, I liked the stuff she was using
I acknowledged her as my dream come true
Making me feel special was all she knew
She influenced my thinking, she eased my pain
A nice pleasant rapport was the vibe we sustained
Her smile would enlighten the darkest night
Everything about this woman felt right
One day suddenly she felt it was time
To end our romance and clear her mind
Without surrendering a goodbye kiss
She considered herself completely dismissed
Understandably, so I have no regrets
I sincerely wish her the absolute best
Gone from my arms in an instant it seemed
Every second with her was like a candid love scene
After all that has happened even still, I proclaim
Thoughts of her on occasions remain

Mother Dear

When I ponder the importance of a mother's love
unconditional is one particular word I think of
dependable and commendable are among others
the word honorable is yet still another
one word my lovely mother rates is endurance
often, she humbled us with reassurance
while affording her attentions towards our various needs
she instilled in our hearts a desire to succeed
at any endeavor we attempted to venture
our mother was a stern and invaluable mentor
my sister MARGIE, brother BRIAN and I
envision her as a hero who is sweet as pie
JACQUELINE GOODING is her name
perseverance and positivity is her claim to fame
the most encouraging woman I acknowledge on earth
is this wonderful angel who conceived our births
Mother for caring for us from the start
you have earned a significant place in our hearts
you showed no signs of hesitation
when we needed you for help
you persistently mastered anticipation
when it came to the way we felt
unselfish were you with your love
when we wanted to be babied
never worrying when push came to shove
you were always shouting, maybe
you are the lady of the hour
when it comes to comfort and understanding
the perfect word for your consistent will power
is that eleven-letter one, "OUTSTANDING"

All Mine

Please consider my desire to chance
a chemistry between us ,can I have this dance
into your heart ,you already have mine
I am interested in spending time
with someone sweet
and somewhat unique
is that someone you
are you feeling me too?
my entire life, where have you been
come on beautiful let me in
pretty you are, as pretty as can be
looking just like you belong to me

Game Over

Our inseparable existence is no fairy tale
her gentle kisses feel real
when a pretty lady romances you well
the connection is a genuine deal
we are experiencing intimate bliss
we are happy as happy can be
my lady Sebrina I must insist
is the right kind of lover for me

It Is I

I am the man who flatters you
with a bevy of pleasant surprises
I concern myself with whatever you do
the second the morning sun rises
I love cozying up to my passion
for wanting and needing you so
it would not be the least bit old fashion
to call me your Romeo

Mirror Image

Mirror, mirror on the wall
who is the most admirable woman of all
that would be mine I would have to insist
the world we live in is sealed with a kiss
stars so bright what a delight
her reflection is that of a gorgeous moonlight
mirror, mirror my exceptional Queen
is the loveliest image you have ever seen

Love

Love is a many splendid thing
Love is the emotional songs we sing
Love is a newborn baby's cry
Love is witnessing a proud mother sigh
Love is a father taking care of his young
Love is a wife saying, "Husband well done"
Love is unconditional, romance between lovers
Love is an eagerness to lend a hand to others
Love is measured, love is treasured
Love is an absolute honorable pleasure
Love is acts of kindness galore
God is love, need I say more

Hearts

I am destined to desire you forever
you are my heart and soul
every single day on this earth feels better
because you are my someone to hold
my favorite reality is holding you tight
while gazing into your eyes to mention
when I am with you I feel so right
without you I feel tension
there is no place left for me to go
except in your arms my dear
consider me hopeless without the flow
of your love to linger me near

Unity

The candle we lit years ago
to secure our acquaintance still burns
yet and still I need you so
for your touch I desperately yearn
the light at the end of the tunnel
can easily be seen
our journey should exceed without stumble
we are a determined team
why should we blow out the fire
and cloud our future with dust
so long as there is desire
there is still hope for us

Distant Lover

Distant lover where are you?
my heart is in despair
I wonder if you would care to
intercept the love I must share
I remember you as the shining star
that sparkled within my heart
your leaving me seemed so bizarre
did you really have to depart?
distant lover where are you?
I am in this lonely room
only you can say it is fair to
exit my thoughts from gloom
I cradle my pillow to my face
overwhelming it with tears
I am finding it hard to swallow the taste
of this sorrowful atmosphere
distant lover where are you?
my pride is slowly fading
hardly am I in the mood
for another day of waiting
time is becoming a bothersome object
I am starting to self-destruct
craving your warmth is my only logic
seeing you is a must
distant lover wherever you are,
I miss you indefinitely
these are my loneliest hours by far
I need you here with me

Special Feelings

I am glad the special love we share
has conjured smiles upon our faces
it is good we are stressing how much we care
although resided in different places
I am missing you everyday
I feel incomplete no doubt
God knows I am not lying when I say
it is you I cannot do without
I see us as that love struck pair
who are miserable when apart
it would be so nice if I were there
to discuss the depths of my heart

Only You

Love with you stays on my mind
I think about it all of the time
a woman like you is hard to find
love with you is discrete
Love with you is like a beautiful dream
like a melody to a soft song theme
like the joy of turning sweet sixteen
love with you is unique
love with you is like living in Heaven
like going to bed with a smile at seven
like waking up in your arms at eleven
love with you is complete
love with you is a God given phase
encouraging enough to keep me amazed
obviously I will love you for days
love with you is sweet

Cheers

She is responsible for the joy in my heart
I could never imagine us growing apart
I would like to propose a toast
to inseparable lovers who are closer than close
our romantic affair is a real big deal
I adore the way she makes me feel
this devoted woman of mine
obliges my every breath
sincerely and yearly I am inclined
to love her until death

Dear Friend

Your smile reflects a sign of charm
steadily glowing with shining honors
your character extends reaching arms
indicating the heart grows fonder
your companionship is appreciated
with hopes it will not be lost
your controversial views are educated
with consideration backing each clause
your handshakes feel extra firm
shielding assurance not likely to end
your counterpart is delighted to learn
he has gained a compatible friend

Honest

The thought of loving another
never even enters my mind
you are my only lover
you deserve all of my time
not once does temptation overtake
my commitment as your one and only man
my motive is to contemplate
every positive emotion I can
I always fail to see
potential other women pursue
without question to any degree
I only have eyes for you

Thank You

How sweet it is to finally find
a woman intently obsessed
with making certain I am confined
and connected with happiness
the lady who relates the story
of ushering her love to her man
is the lady I cherish, to God be the glory
simply because I can

Comfort

I remember the way we were
the passionate tender kisses
I remember all of the emotions we shared
our hopes, our dreams, our wishes
I remember my desires
to hold you ever so tight
I remember you setting my soul on fire
by making me feel so right

Destiny

I have been crying out desperately for you
from the very second you left
I am biting off more than I can chew
this is very hard to accept
let it be said you are the force
surfacing the significance of my well being
your sudden departure has likely endorsed
the sorrow I am foreseeing
dreams of you are not nearly enough
I awaken to find you not there
I cannot rely on a vision of bluffs
your absence from me is not fair
each moment I yearn for your touch
I encounter the urge to cry
oh my darling I need you so much
why are you saying goodbye
I will never stop searching for you
where oh where could you be
imagine the torture you are putting me through
and bring your love back to me

Say Yes

I see us spending quality time
I must confess, if you were mine
the depths of my soul would be yours to take
into happily ever after as your permanent mate
it would be nice if I could embrace
the opportunity to corral your emotions with grace
and style the whole nine yards
my thoughts concerning you are of the highest regard
as far as I am concerned, you are that lady
you think we could develop a relationship "maybe"

I Love You

Every time, I mention these words
I acquire a sensational feeling
holding them in is for the birds
letting them out is fulfilling
especially when I am saying them
to someone I truly care for
there is no point in delaying them
I am more than eager to share more
I live to express what is in my heart
satisfy you with the thought you are needed
while preventing our affections from falling apart
by reassuring you we have succeeded
I no longer desire to prolong the suspense
of whom I am referring to
confronting another woman makes no sense
cause darling, I love only you

It's Me

Realize you have a secret admirer
who is observing you very closely
I can promise you this someone's inspired
by your down to earth persona mostly
the features on your adorable face
settles his mind in a very good place
there is more he is reluctant to mention
he wants you to know you have his attention
the shy admirer who has yet to confess
is certain by now you have probably guessed

Cinderella

This glass shoe is all about you
a future for us is in clear view
my loving inspiration,
my sweet sensation
come to the ball
you have convinced me to fall
for your lovely brown eyes
can we compromise
I want us to be
Are you calling for me
If so, here I stand
vowing to be your man
secure am I and warm in your midst
all is well
the glass slipper fits

She Tried

She was there when you had no friend
to talk to while in distress
she showed no signs of giving in
when you got yourself in a mess
standing by you the entire time
she would often offer her help
multiple times you accused her of lying
when you were out with someone else
now you are wondering why she left
claiming she has done you wrong
plagued by guilt you refuse to accept
you are the reason she's gone
finally, she realized it was no use
trying to salvage a broken home
today you are drooling over this news
tonight, you will be sleeping alone

My Girl

She is the sexiest woman alive
every second with her is perfection realized
she prides herself on loving me good
one thousand times better than any other woman could
together always, the lover's message
is the very reason we have invested
into caring for one another an awful lot
ain't no woman like the one I got

Sebrina

When God created her, he broke the mold
her eyes are the window to my soul
she never ceases to amaze
she is a blessing, I give God praise
her smile is a breathtaking sight to see
she brings out the absolute best in me
loving her unconditionally means everything
this woman of mine makes me feel like a king

Positive Thoughts

The words came quickly, innocently and faithful
yet they sounded so terrific
I meant them, felt them, and needed
to say them the very moment you heard them
my thoughts could not hold them any longer
the moment was right
I said them to surprise you
I said them to assure you
I said them for you
because you deserved to hear them
I said them for me
because I owed it to myself to say them
allow them to touch your heart
I will say them again
I will say them now
"I Love You"

Tears Of Joy

The reason I am emotional today
I love you very much
without you there is no possible way
I can focus without losing touch
you are my queen, my desirable view
the kiss that makes me feel better
spending an entire lifetime with you
completes my world all together
the day you became my Valentine
is the day I began insisting
your precious love is good for my mind
without you I would just be existing

You Are

You are the air I breathe
you are the apple of my eye
happiness is agreeing with me
you are the reason why
you are my beautiful flower
my rainbow in the sky
you are the minutes in my hour
the teardrops that I cry
you are my main attraction
the feature song I sing
speaking with words of action
you are my everything

One Song

The love song in my heart created by you
is a perfect melody suited for two
serenade me all the days of my life
it is my favorite tune, keep me enticed
don't stop singing
my heart is ringing
with joy unreal
what a cool deal
hey sweetest woman I have ever known
come dance with me to this passionate song

What If

What would you do if I confessed?
knowing you astounds me with thrills
am I wrong to become obsessed?
with this attraction for you I feel
how would you handle it if I told you
being with you is what I am needing
would you shy away from my attempts to hold you?
if you thought they were too misleading
would you respond with a negative sigh?
if I proposed a sexual rendezvous,
would you vocally strengthen the word good-bye
when informed I am falling for you?

The Question Is

Are we one meaningful love song away,
of actually becoming carefree
can we bond will we find our way
to devotion, you and me
are we destined, is this our time
am I that man you can trust
I would be honored to call you mine
does romance agree with us

Looking Good

Adoration for you is beginning to be
a reality I cannot control
your complexion's smoothness alerts me
as beauty needing cause to behold
forgive me if I seem precise
but my source for intimate peace
develops the instant I focus my eyes
upon your lovely face "Capiche"

Hot Showers

Show some compassion, kiss my lips
establish with me a relationship
a candlelight dinner for two sounds nice
I could look into your eyes and be enticed
whisper sweet nothings in my ear and relay
flirtatious notions, I might want to play
be amazed with me, become obsessed
fall victim to my soothing caress
shower your affections upon me—hurry
I assure you I am more than worthy

Have You Ever

My attraction for you I will not deny
feels amazing, I am the guy
you can count on to love you madly
my intentions are real I want you badly
I will do whatever it takes to
be the only man who caters to you
honestly having you by my side
would make me the happiest man alive
when you think of lover's bonding together
are you thinking of us or at least have you ever

So Good

Confession, can I be sincere
I am completely calm when you are near
give me you every day of the week
awesome woman who dares to be sweet
can I count on you to be the one
to humble my thoughts Misses second to none
the most romantic story ever told
is intimacy shared by consenting souls
you should consider thinking of
one day becoming my forever love

Always

Always I will choose to be where you are
anywhere possible no matter how far
the reality of our courtship makes me proud
poised I am always to love you out loud
this is about me refusing to stop
cherishing us no matter what
always and forever is necessary
with the woman I intend to marry
the woman who makes me feel brand new
I will always be in love with you

Private Dancer

Oh, how very exciting it is
to share a compatible bond with this
irresistible woman, our quality time
is an awesome experience, this lady of mine
is one of God's brilliant creations
abundant intimacy defines our relation
with soft music playing
I am simply saying
this pleasant woman so endearing so smart
danced her way directly into my heart

My Vow

Loyal to you, I am to life's end
exceptional lady you are a God send
you are always amazing always classy
super intelligent sexy and sassy
anything that makes me smile
most definitely is worth my while
for your sweet love my arms open wide
I never intend to leave your side

The Photographic Message

This absolute gorgeous image of you
is one to forever cherish
its likeness reveals what I already knew
my maiden is the fairest
inspiring is the beautiful face
that requires excessive staring
this photograph lady falls completely in place
with the wonderful thoughts we are sharing
the astonishing portrait clearly exposes
a loving angel in disguise
who easily deserves an arrangement of roses
for being a sight for sore eyes

Just Saying

My answered prayer has finally arrived
you got me feeling all gentle inside
I need you my Cherie Amour
my feelings about us cannot be ignored
It just so happens, I truly believe
you are the perfect woman for me
I have an idea—let's love each other
to the moon and back and never recover

Love Your Woman

Send her roses every once in a while
flatter her with compliments, acknowledge her smile
go out of your way to absolutely adore her
what reason at all would you have to ignore her
become the gentleman she has waited for all life long
slow dance with her to a lovely love song
never stop creating stars in her sky
make her the sparkling diamond you could never deny
cherish your woman with all of your being
and assuredly so you shall begin seeing
the beautiful soul God created for you
should always be made to feel brand new

Matrimony

Upon one knee, I extend my hand
I am asking you to be mine
I promise I am the honorable man
who will treasure you for a lifetime
bond with me, here is the thing—
I am anxious to afford your desires
if you will accept this ring,
my purpose becomes inspired
this proposal has been in existence
from the day our love came to be
ignore the thought of resistance
and say you will marry me

Smooches

I am moonlighting under the stars tonight
pondering thoughts of a romance that felt so right
this lady and I were primed to explore
affections we were eventually forced to ignore
we shared quality time; she once was mine
hopes and wishes, sweet soft kisses
we were a couple in love, naïve, and young
we dared to remain loyal; we blossomed as one
you win some, you lose some—I suppose
that appears to be the way the story goes
still moonlighting amongst the stars so bright
deeply into the still of the night
thinking about the woman who
I once surrendered my kisses to

Emotional Circumstances

Unconditional love is about you and I,
a couple of undeniable forevers
who are satisfied with reasons why
we are amazing together
my sugar, my spice, my everything nice
my lover, my all that I need
I feel like I am in paradise
you mean the world to me

True Love

I feel fortunate my truest love
is an infinite blessing from God above
she means more to me than I have ever dreamed
how encouraging she is for my self esteem
thank you Lord for my perfect gift
to be regarded this way is a spiritual lift
Father in Heaven mission complete
my darling Sebrina is my heartbeat

Sweet Love

Now is our time
desirable lady of mine
realistically, my wonderful dream
is the wedding day featuring you as my queen
falling in love is an undeniable bonus
especially when God is looking down on us
my pleasant surprise
my sight for sore eyes
privileged I am to be the gentleman who
kisses your lips whenever I want to

Greater Is He

As I notice the earthly functions around me
somehow, they focus in to astound me
such as the thunder that trembles the skies
the chirping noises of birds flying by
to witness the steady flow of the sea
is such a glorious moment for me
in church, the most rewarding profile
is the meaningful glow of a Christian smile
when I look out at the stars above,
I notice a refined message of love
the elements of livelihood solace from
an origin of power created by One
some people find these events to be odd,
but they all represent a message from God

Absolutely

I will usher you into a compromising situation
blow your mind—lead you into temptation
make you feel like the queen you are
bring every one of your needs up to par
don't ever doubt me
you would be miserable without me
romance is my game
Ricky Jones is my name
Thanks again ladies and
gentleman for your support
"God bless"

God Is Love

Who am I without my maker
He fed me the breath of life
who am I without my Savior
His brilliance is my light
who am I without the touch
of His spirits to strengthen my thoughts
who am I, am I much
if I slander the sermon He's taught
exclude God, and there is no life
not even the time of day
include Him and the purpose for life
prevails in a positive way
who am I without the conscience
to make my life out of something
without the enlightening presence of God
who am I, I am "nothing"

Amazed

My beautiful woman, my answered prayer
you are always amazing, pretty lady I swear
the definition of torture is existing without
your precious love, I am emphatic about
spoiling you with an arrangement of flowers
for loving me tender for so many hours
much is given, much is required
beautiful woman, you keep me inspired

Candy Girl

Que the horns, my queen is present
gorgeous lady, I admire
the reassuring level of pleasant
you gracefully inspire
your smile, your style, your scent, your touch
are stunning qualities I view
as specific reasons to adore so much
the sweet irreplaceable you

Perfection Realized

I am afforded the luxury of feeling
brand new
I thank God for the wonderful things
you do
to endearingly influence my inner
soul
with a comforting assurance that
makes me feel whole
impressive is your passion to strive
to be
my greatest inspiration voluntarily
my precious lover, you stand alone
as the most admirable woman I
have ever known

Innocent Blessings

we have grown accustomed to
spoiling one another
this joy in my heart is a sacred
discover
thanks to my virtuous shining star
who is perfect for me, my love
yes you are
you captivated my soul, job well
done
the best for us is yet to come
my intuition tells me we would be
wise
to cherish each other for the rest of
our lives

I Adore

I adore the way you love me
thoroughly yet so gentle
your frequent urges to hug me
does wonders for my mental
I adore the way you whisper my name
to tell me you need me so
I adore being the one to blame
for keeping your smile aglow

Thanks so much for reading!
"God Bless You All."

Praise Him

Each morning I awaken with my right mind
immediately I realize I am inclined
to be abundantly blessed and highly
favored
the breath of life is my blessing to savor
God's grace and mercy is my welcomed
reward
I am so grateful, "Thank You Lord"

Acknowledgement

The actual author of this book of poetry is God. He made it possible for me to create each phrase and execute every rhyme. Certainly as always, He is right on time.

"POWER BELONGS TO GOD"

His Glory Creations Publishing, LLC is an International Christian Book Publishing Company, established in 2017, which helps launch the creative fiction and non-fiction works of new, aspiring, and seasoned authors across the globe, through stories that are inspirational, empowering, life changing or educational in nature, including anthologies, poetry, journals, children's books, and audio books.

DESIRE TO KNOW MORE?

Contact Information:
CEO/Founder: Felicia C. Lucas

www.hisglorycreationspublishing.com
Email: hgcpublishingllc@gmail.com
Office Phone: 919-679-1706

Facebook: His Glory Creations Publishing
Instagram: His Glory Creations Publishing
YouTube: His Glory Creations Publishing

www.ingramcontent.com/pod-product-compliance
Lightning Source LLC
Chambersburg PA
CBHW071228160426
43196CB00012B/2451